Abuse of Human Rights of Indian Seafarers

Abuse of Human Rights of Indian Seafarers

Capt. Sanjay Prashar
Vice President-Forum for Integrated National Security (FINS)

Abhishek Malhotra
Law Student and Marine Engineer

Mohamed Abuthahir
Maritime Expert

GYAN

ISBN: 978-81-212-9925-1 (PB)

Published, 2022

Published by

Gyan Publishing House
5, Ansari Road
Daryaganj, New Delhi-110002
Phone: 011-47034999, 9811692060
www.gyanbooks.com
E-mail: books@gyanbooks.com

Printed at: Gyan Press, Delhi.

Contents

Acknowledgement

Good Day! Dear Readers,

I am deeply honoured to be given this opportunity to address this issue which is of paramount importance for the industry and the some is running this country from decades.

I am assiduous in scribing this issue i.e., '**Abuse of Human Rights of Indian Seafarers across the globe**'. Through this booklet, I am enlightening NHRC and Human Rights fraternity with some pragmatic case studies, in which I've immense escapade.

I have veracious belief, that by working on this subject, and rendering shoulder to shoulder support could help us to eradicate 'The Abuse of Human Rights of Indian Seafarers' across the globe. Therefore, let's all take a pledge to be the Protector of Human Rights of each and every citizen on this planet.

Profound and Best Regards Always,

Yours' Truly,
Sanjay Prashar.
Vice President-Forum for Integrated National Security
(FINS)

List of abbreviations used in this book

ACP - Assistant Commissioner of Police
BE - Bachelor of Engineering
BST - Basic Safety Training
CBA - Collective Bargaining Agreement
DGS - Directorate General of Shipping
DMLC - Declaration of Maritime Labour Compliance
DNS - Diploma in Nautical Science
DSEO - Director Seamen's Employment Office Federation
FIR - First Information Report
GME - Graduate Marine Engineering
GOI - Government of India
HMS - Hind Mazdoor Sabha
ILO - International Labour Organisation
IMO - International Maritime Organisation
ITF - International Transport Workers
MEA - Ministry of External Affairs
MLC - Maritime Labour Convention
MOS - Minister of State
MTI - Maritime Training Institute
MUI - Maritime Union of India
NGO - Non-Governmental Organisation
NHRC - National Human Rights Commission
NS - Nautical Science
NUSI - National Union of Seafarers of India

OTP	- One Time Password
PHRA	- Protection of Human Rights Act
PIC	- Person-in-Charge
PNI	- Protection and Indemnity Insurance
POEA	- Protector of Emigrants
RPS	- Recruitment and Placement Services
RPSL	- Recruitment and Placement Services Licence
SEA	- Seafarers Employment Agreement
SHRC	- State Human Rights Commissions
SWFS	- Seafarers Welfare Fund Society
TME	- Trainee Marine Engineer
UDHR	- Universal Declaration of Human Rights

A. Human Rights

The 'human rights' are the rights that are inherent to all human beings, regardless of race, sex, nationality, ethnicity, language, religion, or any other status. Human rights include the right to life and liberty, freedom from slavery and torture, freedom of opinion and expression, the right to work and education, etc.; essential for the very existence of the person as an integral part of the society. Every individual is entitled to these rights without discrimination.

A. I. Human rights -a global standard

The human rights are universal and have to be followed across the world. This has necessitated standardisation of these rights that every nation must protect, in respect for every person that is present within its terrestrial, maritime or aerial jurisdiction.

A. I. 1 International Human Rights law

International human rights law lays down the responsibilities and obligations of Governments to promote and protect human rights and fundamental freedom of individuals or groups- to act in certain ways or to refrain from certain acts.

A universal and internationally protected code to which all nations can subscribe and all people aspire is the creation of a comprehensive body of human rights law formulated by the United Nations. The United Nations has defined a broad range of internationally accepted rights, including civil, cultural, economic, political and social rights. It has also established mechanisms to promote and protect these rights and to assist states in carrying out their responsibilities.

The law is founded on the Charter of the United Nations and the Universal Declaration of Human Rights, adopted by the UN General Assembly in 1945 and 1948, respectively. Over the years, the United Nations has gradually expanded the scope of human rights law, to encompass specific standards for specific categories such as women, children, persons with disabilities, minorities and other vulnerable groups, who now possess the rights that protect them from discrimination, which previously existed in many societies.

A. II. United Nations and Human Rights

The Universal Declaration of Human Rights (UDHR) is perhaps the most important document in defining the human rights; a historic step in many ways.

The declaration was drafted by representatives from all regions of the world with different legal and cultural backgrounds. The 'Declaration' so drafted was adopted by the United Nations General Assembly in Paris on 10 December 1948 vide the General Assembly Resolution 217 A (III); as a common standard that must be achieved by all the nations and for all people. It lays down for the first time, fundamental human rights to be universally protected.

Since its adoption in 1948, the UDHR has inspired the constitutions of many newly independent States and many new democracies. The UDHR, together with the International Covenant on Civil and Political Rights and its two Optional Protocols (on the complaints procedure and on the death penalty) and the International Covenant on Economic, Social and Cultural Rights and its Optional Protocol, comprises the 'International Bill of Human Rights'.

Human rights is a cross-cutting theme in all UN policies and programmes in the key areas of peace and security, development, humanitarian assistance, and economic and social affairs. As a result, virtually every UN body and specialised agency is involved to some degree in the protection of human rights. Some examples are the right to development, which is at the core of the Sustainable Development Goals; the right to food, championed by the UN Food and Agriculture Organisation, labour rights, defined and protected by the International Labour Organisation, gender equality, which is promulgated by UN Women, the rights of children, indigenous peoples, and disabled persons.[1]

A. II. 1 Economic, Social and Cultural Rights

The International Covenant on Economic, Social and Cultural

Rights entered into force in 1976. The human rights that the Covenant seeks to promote and protect include:

- the right to work in just and favourable conditions;
- the right to social protection, to an adequate standard of living and to the highest attainable standards of physical and mental well-being;
- the right to education and the enjoyment of benefits of cultural freedom and scientific progress.

A. II. 2 Civil and Political Rights

The International Covenant on Civil and Political Rights and its First Optional Protocol came into force in 1976. The Second Optional Protocol was adopted in 1989.

The Covenant deals with the following rights:

(a) freedom of movement;

(b) equality before the law;

(c) the right to a fair trial and presumption of innocence;

(d) freedom of thought, conscience and religion;

(e) freedom of opinion and expression; peaceful assembly;

(f) freedom of association; participation in public affairs and elections; and

(g) protection of minority rights.

It also prohibits arbitrary deprivation of life; torture, cruel or degrading treatment or punishment; slavery and forced labour; arbitrary arrest or detention; arbitrary interference with privacy; war propaganda; discrimination; and advocacy of racial or religious hatred.

A. II. 3 Human Rights Conventions

A series of international human rights treaties and other instruments have been adopted since 1945 to strengthen the international human rights law. They include, the Convention on the Prevention and Punishment of the Crime of Genocide (1948), the International Convention on the Elimination of All Forms of Racial Discrimination (1965), the Convention on the Elimination of All Forms of Discrimination against Women (1979), the Convention on the Rights of the Child (1989) and the Convention on the Rights of Persons with Disabilities (2006), among others.

A. II. 4 Human Rights Council

The Human Rights Council (UN-HRC), the key UN intergovernmental body responsible for human rights was established on 15 March 2006 by the General Assembly and reporting directly to it. UN-HRC replaced the 60-year-old UN Commission on Human Rights as. The Council is made up of 47 State representatives and is tasked with strengthening the promotion and protection of human rights around the globe by addressing situations of human rights violations and making recommendations on them, including responding to human rights emergencies.

The Human Rights Council conducts the Universal Periodic Review, which involves a review of the human rights records of all 193 UN member states once every four years. The Review is a cooperative, state-driven process, under the auspices of the Council, which provides the opportunity for each state to present measures taken and challenges to be met to improve the human rights situation in their country and to meet their international obligations. The Review is designed to ensure universality and equality of treatment for every country.

A. II. 5 UN High Commissioner for Human Rights

The United Nations High Commissioner for Human Rights is primarily responsible for UN human rights activities. The High Commissioner is mandated to respond to serious violations of human rights and to undertake preventive action.

The Office of the High Commissioner for Human Rights (OHCHR) is the focal point for United Nations human rights activities. It serves as the secretariat for the Human Rights Council, the expert committees that monitor treaty compliance (known as treaty bodies) and other UN human rights organs. It also undertakes human rights field activities.

Most of the core human rights treaties have an oversight body which is responsible for reviewing the implementation of that treaty by the countries that have ratified it. Individuals, whose rights have been violated can file complaints directly to Committees overseeing human rights treaties.

A. III. Human Rights protection-Indian perspective

The constitution of India enshrines the protection of human rights under the 'Fundamental Rights' of its citizens. These 'inter alia' include the following:

(a) Right to equality irrespective of race, religion, caste, gender or place of birth.

(b) Equality of opportunity in respect of public employment.

(c) Freedom of

- speech and expression,
- move freely throughout the territory,
- reside and settle anywhere in India,
- to practise any profession, or to carry on any occupation, trade or business.

(d) Protection of life and personal liberty.

(e) Right to education,

(f) Freedom of conscience and the right to freely profess, practise and propagate religion.

(g) Prohibition of child labour.

India is one of the 193 member states of the UN-HRC.

A. III. 1 National Human Rights Commission- NHRC[2]

The National Human Rights Commission (NHRC) of India was established on 12 October, 1993, under the Protection of Human Rights Act (PHRA), 1993, passed by the Parliament of India. The act was amended by the Protection of Human Rights (Amendment) Act, 2006.

It is in conformity with the Paris Principles, adopted at the first international workshop on national institutions for the promotion and protection of human rights held in Paris in October 1991, and endorsed by the General Assembly of the United Nations by its Regulations 48/134 of 20 December, 1993.

The NHRC is an embodiment of India's concern for the promotion and protection of human rights.

Section 2(1)(d) of the PHRA defines Human Rights as the rights relating to life, liberty, equality and dignity of the individual guaranteed by the Constitution or embodied in the International Covenants and enforceable by courts in India.

The objective of the commission formed under the act is the protection and promotion of human rights. The functions of the Commission as stated in Section 12 of the Act and apart from enquiry into complaints of violation of human rights or negligence in the prevention of such violation by a public servant, the Commission also studies treaties and international instruments on human rights and make recommendations for their effective implementation to the Government.

The Commission is responsible for spreading of human rights awareness amongst the masses and encouraging the efforts of all stake holders in the field of human rights literacy not only at the national level but at the international level too. NHRC is a unique institution because it is one of the few National Human Rights Institutes (NHRIs) in the world, whose Chairperson is the former Chief Justice of the country. The NHRC of India serves as a role model in promoting and monitoring effective implementation of promotion and protection of human rights.

Section 2(1) (d) of the PHR Act defines Human Rights as the rights relating to life, liberty, equality and dignity of the individual guaranteed by the Constitution or embodied in the International Covenants and enforceable by courts in India.

SOME important SECTIONS OF PHRA, 1993

Section 2 (1) (d) Definition of "Human Rights"

Section 3 Constitution of National Human Rights Commission

Section 12 Functions of the Commission

Section 13 Powers relating to inquires

Section 14 Investigation

Section 17 Inquiry in complainants

Section 21 Constitution of State Human Rights Commission

Section 30 Human Rights Courts

A. IV. Human Rights Legislation relating to Seafarers

The seafarers, by virtue of the very nature of employment, move from country to country during their occupation. The Seafarers are in many ways, a unique category of people who are thus exposed to the laws of different countries on a continuous basis.

The maritime jurisdiction of a country extends upto an area of 12 nautical miles from the shores of the country. Consequently, that nation's human rights law applies to the seafarers when within that jurisdiction.

However, the human rights of the seafarers must also be protected when in international waters. Considering the peculiar position of the seafarers aboard the ships that fly flags of different countries, it was felt that the seafarers have not been adequately protected and are extremely vulnerable because they are beyond the jurisdiction of the States that bear responsibility for their protection.

The issue of maritime human rights protection for all persons living, working, transiting, or engaged in any other type of activity at sea in territorial and international waters around the globe, thus assumed great importance.

A. IV. 1 The Geneva Declaration

In order to protect the human rights at sea, the Geneva Declaration on Human Rights at Sea was proclaimed on 15th April 2019.

A. IV. 1. (a) Preamble of Geneva Declaration

The preamble of the declaration[3] states-

Activity at sea, both legitimate and unlawful, is increasing year-on-year. This is leading to an increase in the global maritime population, currently estimated to be around 40-50 million people: men, women and children. The majority of these are fishers, approximately 30 million, an estimated 20,000 of whom are children working at sea and in coastal fishing industries. Others are at sea in the shipping industry, in offshore oil and gas industries, engaging in tourism and a range of other activities. Importantly, there are also increasing numbers using the seas and oceans as a means of migration, including in unregulated and trafficked circumstances. The presence, in increasing numbers of people on the seas and oceans, generates a growing need for their protection against threats to their basic human rights. Human rights apply to the same extent at sea as they do on land, in theory, nobody is in a human rights vacuum. Sadly, however, it is a harsh fact that not all those at sea find themselves under the effective jurisdiction of States capable of protecting their human rights. The result is, that a great many who are vulnerable end up being abused, with those doing the abusing escaping the consequences of their actions. There is significant and growing evidence of the systematic abuse of human rights at sea. As examples, those abused include the following:

- Fishers held in slavery on fishing grounds thousands of miles away from where they were 'recruited'.
- Those being trafficked into sexual slavery, thousands attempting to transit oceans to escape conflict and discrimination, or simply in search of better lives for themselves and their families, but paying unscrupulous traffickers in the process.
- Seafarers abandoned by shipping interests who no longer have a reason to employ them, and leaving them without pay or compensation on a foreign shore.
- Those working legitimately within the shipping industry, but experiencing deprivation of their human and basic employment rights.
- Victims of sexual assault on board passenger carrying vessels, including very large cruise ships carrying thousands of passengers, and operating under the flags of states having no means of monitoring or ensuring compliance with human rights standards.

People are disappearing at sea, they are dying at sea, they are being assaulted and abused. If this were occurring ashore, within the territory of a State, it would be well publicised but, because it is happening at sea, on the oceans and out of sight of land, those who could act to stop it are often oblivious to the problem. Unfortunately, even if known about, serious human rights abuses are not easily policed at sea.

There is a serious lack of forces capable of enforcing the law at sea, even within coastal regions. On the high seas, where no State exercises territorial jurisdiction, it is frequently almost impossible to identify which States bear principal responsibility for human rights violations. It is worrying that States that could act, far too frequently seem to use this as an excuse to turn a blind eye.

A. IV. 1. (b) Aim of the declaration

The principal aim of the Geneva Declaration is to raise global awareness of the abuse of human rights at sea and to mobilise a concerted international effort to put an end to it.

The declaration recognises that people at sea are full beneficiaries of human rights, the fact that they may be at sea beyond the limits of territorial jurisdiction does not affect their rights.

There is a profound need for the concept of 'Human Rights at Sea' to be accepted globally. It is primarily the States that have responsibility for enforcing human rights standards at sea. Other actors, international organisations, non-governmental organisations, private companies, masters of vessels, security personnel on-board vessels, and civil society bodies also need to recognise and accept their own roles in the protection of human rights at sea.

Enforcing human rights standards at sea is problematic, with the territorial jurisdiction of States only extending to 12 nautical miles from the shore. Well over 60% of the Earth's surface (being covered with oceans) is therefore, beyond the limits of States' territory.

If human rights at sea are to be respected, complied with, and enforced, all States need to accept their extraterritorial responsibilities on the oceans. There can be no safe and secure legal order for the seas and oceans, if human rights are not enjoyed by all people at sea, and there can be no enjoyment if violations are not effectively addressed, and those affected are not provided with an effective remedy.

A. IV. 2 Human Rights at Sea

Human rights are universal; they apply not only on land but at sea as well. Human rights apply to all individuals, regardless of race, religion, nationality, colour, sex, language, social origin, occupation, political or other opinion, etc. The 2011 UN Guiding Principles on Business and Human Rights[4], reflect human rights at sea.

The seas and oceans are a public space, which provides for movement of vessels and people from all States, and different States, exercise their jurisdiction based on the admiralty jurisdiction.

Maintaining the order of the oceans, including the protection of human rights at seas, is a collective responsibility of the international community. The 'international community' consists of individual States, all of whom are responsible for their share of the international community's 'collective responsibility' for human rights at sea. States also need to act independently as well as collectively, when necessary. Particularly, the States flag of which the ships fly, coastal States and port States need to act to ensure effective protection of human rights at sea, for all people. Appropriate remedial measures must be prescribed and available, if their rights are infringed, breached or abused in any manner whatsoever. Unfortunately, the seas and oceans have not been the focus of human rights processes to the same extent as States ashore.

The concept of Human Rights at Sea encompasses the human rights issues at sea, of raising global awareness of the problem, and of highlighting the need for concerted international action.

This Declaration reflects existing and established international law and principles. No new law is necessary to establish the fundamental principles of human rights at sea. Those fundamental principles already exist, but they are not universally respected, they are not universally complied with, nor are they adequately enforced.

While the seas are a challenging environment and have unique characteristics that demand unique responses, this emphatically does not mean that human rights standards can be compromised in any way. While effective remedy is difficult to achieve in relation to human rights at sea, the ultimate aim of this Declaration is to ensure that it ought to be achieved. The seas are free for all legitimate use; this is an established principle of customary international law and it has been enshrined in the 1982 UN Convention on the Law of the Sea. The stress is on legitimate use. The abuse of human rights at sea is not a legitimate use of the seas in any circumstance. Safe, secure and well-ordered oceans are essential for the international community to enjoy the use and resources of the oceans in a responsible and sustainable manner.

The protection of human rights and their enforcement at sea does not threaten or undermine the free use of the oceans. On the contrary, it is an essential means of ensuring that free use is maintained effectively whilst human rights standards and protections are upheld.

A. IV. 3 The Fundamental Principles

The concept of human rights at sea rests on the following four Fundamental principles:

A. Human rights apply at sea to exactly the same degree and extent that they do on land.

B. All persons at sea, without any distinction, enjoy human rights at sea.

C. There are no maritime specific rules allowing derogation from human rights standards.

D. All human rights established under treaty and customary International law must be respected at sea.

Notes

1. https://www.un.org/en/global-issues/human-rights
2. https://nhrc.nic.in
3. https://www.humanrightsatsea.org
4. https://www.unglobalcompact.org/library/2

B. Human Rights of Seafarers- an Indian Perspective

As per International Maritime Organisation (IMO), international shipping transports more than 80% of global trade, delivering to people and communities all over the world. There are about 100,000 merchant ships sailing globally with about 20,00,000 Seafarers employed on-board.

Shipping is the most efficient and cost-effective means of international transportation for most goods; it provides a dependable, low-cost means of transporting goods globally, facilitating commerce and helping to create prosperity among nations and people.

As per International Chamber of Shipping, globally there are about 65,000 Merchant Ships with about 1.2 million serving on them.

In the Year 2018, about two lac Indians were employed as Seafarers– highest ever in our history. About 87% of these were employed on foreign flag merchant ships and 13% on Indian Flag ships.

The no. of Indian seafarers is expected to see 35% increased employment in the year 2019 only on Foreign Flag ships.

Growth in number of Indian Seafarers-

Year	2013	2014	2015	2016	2017	2018
Rank						
A) Nautical Officers	26742	28805	30520	33346	34417	40897
B) Nautical Ratings	36910	44548	49144	56916	63520	97703
C) Engineering Officers	26995	28968	31377	35260	36760	44388
D) Engineering Ratings	13188	14769	15904	18448	19652	25811
E) Total Officers- A+C	53737	57773	61897	68606	71177	85285
F) Total Ratings-B+D	50098	59317	65048	75364	83172	123514
G) Total Seafarers E+F	103835	117090	126945	143970	154349	208799

India being a Seafarers supplying nation, has seen 300% growth of Indian Seafarers in last 10 years.

According to data published by ILO[1], 137 Indian Seafarers were stranded on ships as on 15th January 2021- highest among those stranded on ships. About 200 Indian Seafarers were reported to have been lodged in various jails.

B. I. Nature of Human Rights Violations against Seafarers

The nature of violation of human rights of seafarers can be broadly categorised as under:

1. Violation of Human Rights on shore.
2. Violation of Human Rights at Sea.

B. I. 1 Violation of Human Rights on Shore

- During pre-sea training
- Detaining and jailing the seafarers in jails without giving sufficient opportunity and time, for petitions in defence being heard. (Denial of principles of natural justice)
- No shore leave
- Unfair treatment of Seafarers (like Crew Change not allowed for Ship crew etc.)

(Each one of the above needs to be explained in detail in the following paras with reference to cases detailed under subsequent chapter)

B. I. 1. (a) During pre-sea training

B. I. 1. (a) 1 Violations by unauthorised Maritime Training Institutes

The training institutes (MTIs) of seafarers have to be approved by DG-shipping. There are more than 100 training institutes with total annual intake is estimated at around 10,000 students. However, many of these institutes do not have DG-Shipping approval and there are many instances of students getting trapped by illegal agents for training in such non-approved MTIs. Such Institutes display flashy websites and misguide youth into Merchant Navy training. Wrong information is given in advertisement by these MTIs.

Such institutes charge hefty fees of INR 3 Lakh for 4 months course. Yet, the skills imparted are absolutely inferior and their students find it difficult to get employment after completion of the course; consequently, the youth become prone to more cheating by Commission Agents and / or consultants in villages and smaller towns.

An indicative list of websites of some of the non-recognised institutes is as under:

http://www.redoceanship.in/
http://www.marinamaritimeacademy.com
https://www.mnavynms.com/
http://merchantnavyrajasthan.com/
https://north-eastern-management-of-seaaffairs.business.site/
http://asiamaritimeacademyvns.com/
http://www.delhiacademy.in/
http://amerkanpur.com/courses.html

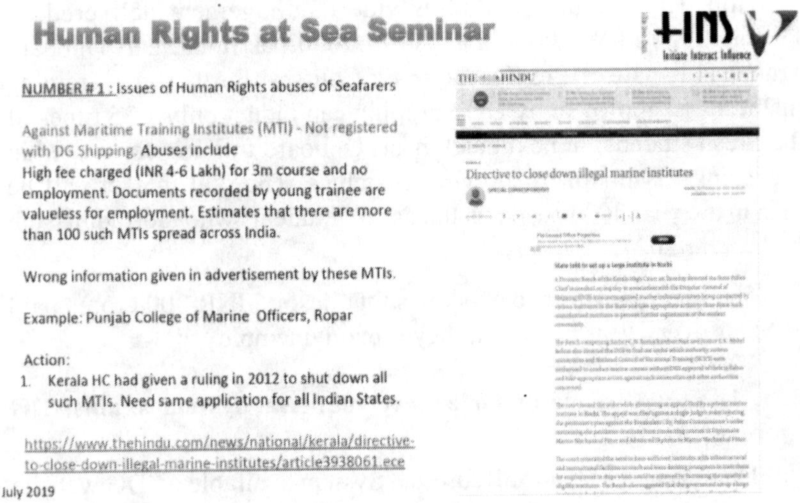

Issues of Human Rights abuses of Seafarers Against Maritime Training Institutes (MTI) - Not registered with DG Shipping, charging high fees (INR 4-6 Lakh) for Course of 3 Months duration and no employment post course completion; is the most important case of human rights violation of seafarers on shore.

Kerala HC had given a ruling in 2012 to shut down all such MTIs in the state. It is necessary that the same be applicable for all Indian States.

B. I. 1. a. 2 Abuse by DG-S approved institutes

Abuses by such institutes include no Job placement after training. As per 2020 data available on DGS Website placement for GP Rating course is 33%, B. Sc. (NS) course is 29%, BE (Marine) course is 49%, DNS (1 year course) is 64% and GME (1 year course) is 67%

Thus, after spending the course fee, the young trainee Seafarers are left to illegal / legal placement agencies to further abuse them. A new type of abuse going on these days is where the illegal agents have direct tie up with the MTIs- the agents charge around 4 lacks as course fees from the trainees whereas the actual fee charged by the MTI is INR 2 lacks. Such agents also promise to pay the entire fees of the candidate but after paying part fees, they disappear. This is well known to the institutes and candidates fear negative impact if they report such matters to authorities. Thus, candidates end up paying double fees.

Hon. High Court of Madras vide its Judgement delivered on 18 Aug 2020 in WP 9050 and 9119 / 2020 has ruled that 'Onboard Training' is part of Pre-Sea Training Courses. Further, the Training Institutes as approved by DG Shipping can induct only 1.25 times of the Fresh students in next batch basis Onboard training completed in preceding 12 month for previous batch/es. The real impact will be seen in the year 2023 based on the data of students who took admission in the year 2021.

The unemployment data shows that despite INR 300 crores paid to MTIs every year by youth, they remain unemployed.

B. I. 1. a. 3 Absence of Grievance redressal system against DG approved MTIs

There is no Grievance Redressal System available on DG website on which the candidates can raise any grievance against the MTIs.

Many a times local police refuse to register FIR in cases of cheating of the student seafarer by the illegal agent.

B. I. 1. a. 4 Other forms of HR abuse of seafarers

B. I. 1. a. 4. i Poor implementation of advertising standards

Poor implementation of the advertising guidelines as given by DG Shipping. Violation of Advertisement guidelines is very frequent and rampant. Absence of any periodic vigilance by the concerned authority on these MTIs in relation to unemployment.

B. I. 1. a. 4. ii False sponsorship

False Sponsorship letter by Recruitment and placement agencies or a sponsorship letter based on 3 Lakh fee which is not honoured by RPS agency is an organised crime perpetrated by the agents with some MTIs that are approved by DG Shipping.

B. I. 1. a. 4. iii Abuse during placement by recruitment agencies

- Fake entries made in DG Shipping system (like Form -1) or E-Migrate to cheat Seafarers. Malicious intent is to take service charges from INR 30K – INR 4 Lakh per seafarer.
- DG Shipping approved 425 RPS (Recruitment and Placement Service) agencies under the Maritime Labour Convention cannot charge any placement fee or service charges. Nevertheless, some RPS agencies take service charges to the tune of INR 2-4 Lakh per placement for fresher and at time for Honduras COC holders; according to records available with DG Shipping Online Grievance Redressal System.
- Seafarers especially fresher's (age group 19 Yrs – 25 Yrs) or first timers are given ship details by RPS agencies and same is stated in FORM 1 of DG Shipping. However, Seafarers are sent to smaller ships and at times on Junk ships which have no Insurance. This results in further abuses of Human Rights at Sea. Iran, Malaysia (SIBU), Nigeria, UAE sees most such cases.
- Seafarers Employment Agreement (SEA) is signed at last minute near airport and seafarers are pushed to take flight. Non-Compliant SEA is noted by Seafarers only upon ship. SEA has to be compliant with MLC 2006 as per DG Shipping RPS rules for all RPS agencies.
- Social media is extensively used by illegal and cheats to attract gullible youth to join Ships. Money is collected from youth in the name of merchant Navy (INR 3 Laks per Seafarer is the rate now-a-days). After that illegal agent changes his phone number.

Seafarer Sanjay Prashar helps repatriate 58 Indian fishermen stranded in Iran

Ananth.MK@timesgroup.com

The fishermen started from Assaluyeh to Tehran on road in two buses on Monday. They will cover around 1,300km on road before they catch the flight from Tehran on Tuesday night and reach Delhi in the early hours of Wednesday

Madurai: Fifty-eight Indian fishermen (40 from Tamil Nadu and 18 from Kerala) working in Iran are stranded after 680 fellow fishermen were repatriated in INS Jalashwa in the last week of June. While the fellow fishermen reached Tuticorin on July 1, completed the mandatory quarantine and returned home, these left out fishermen faced a lot of hardships as their exit visa was stamped and their ex-employers were not ready to take them back.

After a lot of struggles, they have managed to reach Assaluyeh and stayed in three rooms. They were unable to arrange for ₹25,000 needed for a flight to India as they had not been to work for more than four months and their families were clueless about arranging the money as the men in Iran were the sole bread winners. L Praveen, general secretary, Maritime People Welfare Association, Chennai, came across their plight.

Knowing that Captain Sanjay Prashar from Himachal Pradesh, chairman of International Maritime Federation (IMF), helped many seafarers return home, Praveen reached out to him on Twitter on July 1. The latter readily agreed to help the fishermen and sponsored their travel costs. He also travelled from Himachal Pradesh to Delhi to meet cabinet minister (for Jal Shakti) Gajendra Singh Shekhawat on the issue on July 6.

"I handed over the list of 58 fishermen and sought his intervention of the government to expedite the clearance of the documents. On the minister's order the government machinery cleared the papers, got the e-passes and logistics required. On July 10, we paid the charge for the chartered flight from Tehran to Delhi. The fishermen will fly from Tehran on Tuesday night and reach Delhi in the early hours of Wednesday," he said.

Congress leader and Thiruvananthapuram MP Shashi Tharoor congratulated Sanjay Prashar on twitter for his noble effort and thanked him for covering tickets of the fishermen stranded in Iran. "Sanjay Prashar has come out of the way to help our men, bore the tickets and also worked on the repatriation process," says activist Charles Johnson who is coordinating the repatriation of 700 odd Indian fishermen from Iran since February.

The fishermen started from Assaluyeh to Tehran on road in two buses on Monday evening and are expected to cover around 1,300km on road before they catch the flight to Delhi at 10.45pm on Tuesday. Mohamed Abuthahir, Chennai branch manager of Sanjay Prashar's company.

These 58 Fisherman were mainly stranded at Port *Assaluyeh* and are being brought by Bus to Tehran, 1400 Kms Journey.

It's time for Government also to think the legality of such business whereby Indians human rights are violated.

Mr Ujjwal Chaudhary from Mumbai and Mr Mohamed Abuthahir from Chennai and Mr L Praveen from Chennai are coordinating with Fisherman and Indian Embassy at Tehran.

Family of Fishermen Premans place who came from Iran

Tamil Nadu 12 fishermen went for fishing in three boats 4 in each boats from Saudi and while returning from Saudi they need to cross from a channel where they encounter three countries waters Saudi, Iran & Kuwait so while crossing that channel Iranian Navy came and arrested them all for illegal entry into waters on 25 May 2020 in that 12 Tamil Nadu Fishermen.

From Saudi Batch - 4 Fishermen are came back by 1st batch on 30 Sep 2020 and another 4 Fishermen are came by 2nd batch on 19 Oct 2020 and 4 Fishermen will be remaining in Iran jail.

Indian 10 Fishermen Released from Myanmar jailed due to border crossing of Andaman Island came to India on 02 Dec 2021 - Arrested on 15 Apr 2021 at Andaman Sea , Capt Sanjay Prashar has helped to get them back to India.

6 • நாகர்கோவில் 29.11.2021

23 மீனவ அமைப்புகள்

மத்திய மீன்வளத் துறை அமைச்சருடன் சந்திப்பு

[illegible]

• மத்திய மீன்வளத்துறை அமைச்சர் புருஷோத்தமன் ருபாலாவை மீனவர் அமைப்பினர் சந்தித்து மனு அளித்தனர்.

தமிழ்நாடு புதுச்சேரி அந்தமான் நிக்கோபார் ஐலண்ட் 23 மீனவ அமைப்புகள் தில்லியில் மத்திய அமைச்சருடன் சந்திப்பு

[illegible]

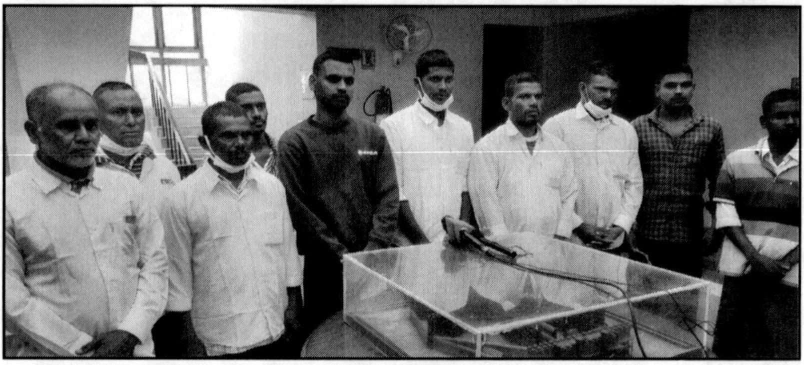

B. I. 1. b Detaining and Jailing of Seafarers

There are many instances of seafarers (particularly fishermen) being jailed by other neighbouring countries without following due process of law.

B. I. 2 Violation of Human Rights at Sea

VIOLATION OF HUMAN RIGHTS ON SEAS include the following:

- Non-payment of wages to seafarers on time.
- No firm policy to deal with the issues of Abandonment / Stranded seafarers.
- Non-Compliance of MLC 206 on board.
- Minuscule Compensation or NO Compensation in case of Death on board.
- No compensation for disability whilst incurring disability when working on board Ships.
- Seafarers Employment Agreement not in line with MLC 2006. Thus, Seafarers are forced to sign such a document at Airport in a rush.

(Each one of the above needs to be explained in detail in the following paras with reference to cases detailed under subsequent chapter)

Note

1. https://www.ilo.org/dyn/seafarers/seafarersBrowse.list?p_lang=en

C. Human Rights Violation- Grievance Redressal Mechanism

नौवहन महानिदेशालय
Directorate General of Shipping
Ministry of Ports, Shipping and Waterways
Government of India

In today's trend, the grievance of the seafarer can be addressed online by logging into his e-governance page, and by launching online grievance to Shipping Master through DGS Website. Following is the list of 7 grievances, on which seafarer can launch his grievance/s online, and can track the status report online only as per DGS, MLC 2006 compliance:

1. Non-Payment of Wages
2. Cases of abandonment
3. Non-compliance of MLC 2006 onboard
4. Death / Missing / Accident
5. Case of Indiscipline by Indian Seafarers

Human Rights at Sea Seminar

FINS
Initiate Interact Influence

NUMBER # 3 : 400 RPS (Recruitment and placement service) Agencies approved by DG shipping & about 100 RPS Agencies Lic cancelled/ suspended / withdrawn / surrendered.

7 types of Grievances as per DGS, MLC 2006 compliance:

1. Non Payment of Wages
2. Cases of abandonment
3. Non compliance of MLC 2006 onboard
4. Death / Missing / Accident
5. Case of Indiscipline by Indian Seafarers
6. Case of Marine Casualty / Medical attention / Repatriation / payment of compen-sation
7. Absconding at Foreign ports

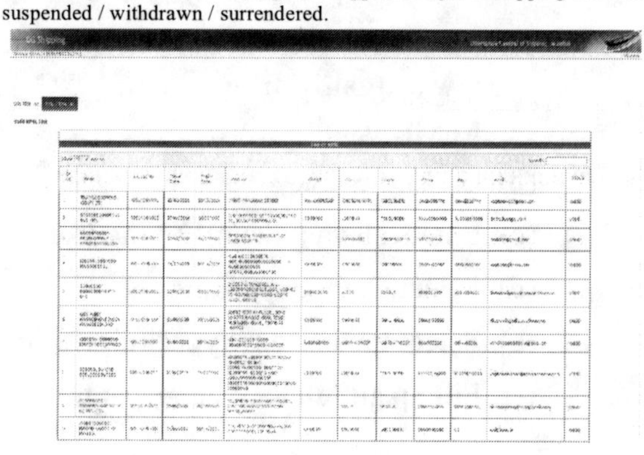

6. Case of Marine Casualty / Medical attention / Repatriation / Payment of Compensation
7. Absconding at Foreign Ports.

C. I. Procedure to launch grievances

C. I. 1 Grievances redressal by DG shipping

Detailed procedure to launch grievances on the DG Shipping "Seafarers' Grievance Redressal Mechanism" is enunciated hereunder:

1. Possible means of receipt of "Seafarers Grievances" may be by any one or more of the following means:
   (a) DGS Online grievance portal
   (b) Email
   (c) Twitter
   (d) Hard copy (letter)
   (e) Social media (as Whatsapp, Twitter etc.)
2. On receipt of grievance by means other than the "Online grievance portal", such as Emails, Tweet, Hard copy (letter) and Social-media etc.; the concerned seafarer who has raised grievance by other means may be advised by email or call by DG Shipping Official / Shipping Master, to raise the grievance through the "DGS Online grievance portal" for quick and easy disposal of case online.
3. Step by step process guide for raising online grievance:
   (a) Login to E-Governance system by using User Id and Password provided by DG

       Shipping E-Governance for other modules www.dgshipping.gov.in "Grievance Redressal Mechanism"
   (b) Go to the link
   (c) Enter relevant details (* marks details are compulsory)
   (d) Select Company Name
   (e) Select the option "type" of grievance
   (f) Fill up all relevant details and 'Submit'

(g) Upon submission of data, system would display "Reference No." and same application would be sent to the concerned "Shipping Master"

(h) The concerned "Shipping Master" would examine the matter within 48 hours and provide necessary solutions

(i) Seafarer can "view" the status of grievance by clicking "view" status

(j) Grievances would be queried back within 48 hours with details or closure

(k) If queried back requesting further details, the same may be provided by the seafarer

(l) If grievances are un-answered, you may contact the respective jurisdictional Shipping Masters by following email id after 48 hours:

- sm-mum-ship@gov.in for Mumbai,
- sm-kol-ship@gov.in for Kolkata,
- sm-chn-ship@gov.in for Chennai

राष्ट्रीय मानव अधिकार आयोग, भारत
NATIONAL HUMAN RIGHTS COMMISSION, INDIA

C. I. 2 FILING A COMPLAINT TO NHRC / SHRC

The Grievance/s of the seafarer/s can also be submitted to NHRC/ SHRC (online) by logging into the below mentioned address:

https://nhrc.nic.in/complaints/complaints/how-tofile-a-complaints

After filing the following data, the complainant can file / keep a vigil, on his complaint filed to NHRC/SHRC.

- Select Incident State.
- Where do you want to submit your complaint.
  (Select NHRC/SHRC).
- Verify your mobile number, through One Time Password (OTP).
- After successfully verification, fill all the mandatory fields on next screen.

- Click preview to finalise your complaint.
- Upload document, if required (PDF Only).
- Select whether you want to show victim and complainant name on website or not.
- After successful submission, you will get a Unique Diary Number.
- Using this Diary number, you can track your complaint status.
- Mandatory fields- fields marked with (*) are mandatory to be filled.

Furthermore, the complainant can also call at toll free number 14433, in case; s/he is unable to file the complaint online.

C. I. 3 Writing to Dept. of Administrative Reforms and Public Grievances

The redressal grievance flow chart for filing a complaint online to https://pgportal.gov.in/Signin, Dept. of Administrative Reforms & Public Grievance, Ministry of Personnel, Public Grievance & Pensions, Government of India.

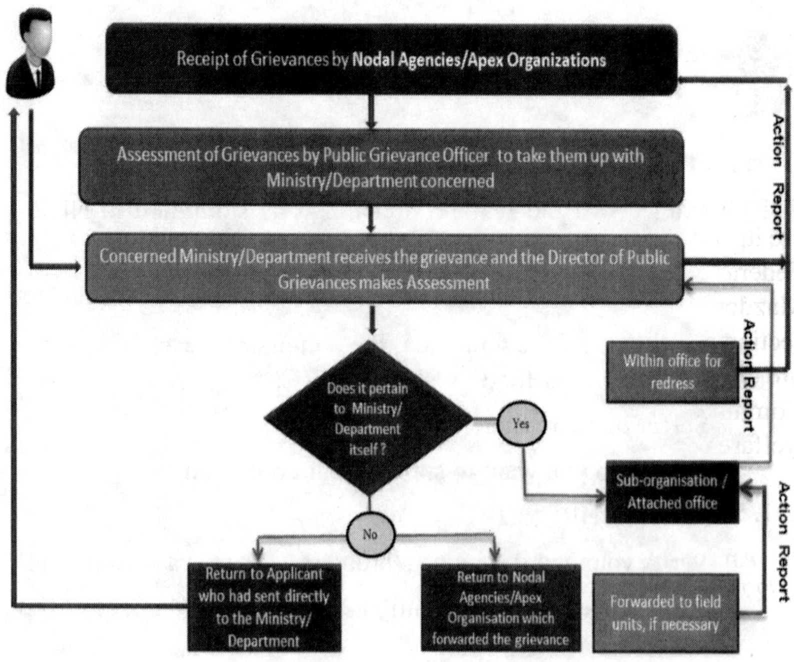

C. I. 4 Seeking Support of Seafarers' National/International Union

Every Country has Seafarers union, which is recognised by Govt bodies or by Industry. In India, there are two such Unions.

NUSI National Union of Seafarers of India

National Union of Seafarers of India (NUSI- https://www.nusi.org.in/) was formed in 1896. NUSI is known for the dedicated services it provides to the seafarers and their families in particular and the Indian shipping in general. It caters to Indian Ratings and petty officers who are working on Off-shore, Home Trade and Foreign going vessels. NUSI is affiliated to the Hind Mazdoor Sabha (HMS) and the International Transport Workers Federation (ITF), London. On issues common to the interest of Officers and Petty Officers, Ratings, NUSI along with the Maritime Union of India (MUI) is together as the Indian Seafarers Federation (ISF).

MUI The Maritime Union of India

represents the Merchant Navy Officers who are members of this Union

The Maritime Union of India (MUI- https://maritimeunionofindia.com) represents Merchant Navy Officers who are its members. It's affiliated to the International Transport Workers' Federation (ITF), London, U.K. MUI is also affiliated to the Hind Mazdoor Sabha (HMS), New Delhi, which represents a very large section of workers from various industries in India. MUI is represented on Government and Semi Government Maritime Boards and Committees. They also liaise with seafarer training institutes and welfare organisations.

C. I. 5 Invoking the Jurisdiction of Courts'

An aggrieved seafarer can invoke the writ jurisdiction under Article 32/226 of the Constitution of India.

C. I. 5. a The Supreme Court of India

Article of the Constitution of India, if any of the fundamental rights are violated, then the person can invoke the jurisdiction of Hon'ble Supreme Court of India. Article 32 of the Constitution of India is reproduced herein:

32. Remedies for enforcement of rights conferred by this Part

(1) The right to move the Supreme Court by appropriate proceedings for the enforcement of the rights conferred by this Part is guaranteed

(2) The Supreme Court shall have power to issue directions or orders or writs, including writs in the nature of habeas corpus, mandamus, prohibition, quo-warranto and certiorari, whichever may be appropriate, for the enforcement of any of the rights conferred by this Part

(3) Without prejudice to the powers conferred on the Supreme Court by clause (1) and (2), Parliament may by law empower any other court to exercise within the local limits of its jurisdiction all or any of the powers exercisable by the Supreme Court under clause (2)

(4) The right guaranteed by this article shall not be suspended except as otherwise provided for by this Constitution.

C. I. 5. b The High Courts

Under Article 226/227 of the Constitution of India, one can invoke the writ jurisdiction of High Courts:

Article 226. Power of High Courts to issue certain writs

(1) Notwithstanding anything in Article 32 every High Court shall have powers, throughout the territories in relation to which it exercises jurisdiction, to issue to any person or authority, including in appropriate cases, any government, within those territories directions, orders or writs, including writs in the nature of habeas corpus, mandamus, prohibitions, quo-warranto and certiorari, or any of them, for the enforcement of any of the rights conferred by Part III and for any other purpose.

(2) The power conferred by clause (1) to issue directions, orders or writs to any government, authority or person may also be exercised by any High Court exercising jurisdiction in relation to the territories within which the cause of action, wholly or in part, arises for the exercise of such power, notwithstanding that the seat of such government or authority or the residence of such person is not within those territories.

(3) Where any party against whom an interim order, whether by way of injunction or stay or in any other manner, is made on, or in any proceedings relating to, a petition under clause (1), without

(a) furnishing to such party copies of such petition and all documents in support of the plea for such interim order; and

(b) giving such party an opportunity of being heard, makes an application to the High Court for the vacation of such order and furnishes a copy of such application to the party in whose favour such order has been made or the counsel of such party, the High Court shall dispose of the application within a period of two weeks from the date on which it is received or from the date on which the copy of such application is so furnished, whichever is later, or where the High Court is closed on the last day of that period, before the expiry of the next day afterwards on which the

High Court is open; and if the application is not so disposed of, the interim order shall, on the expiry of that period, or, as the case may be, the expiry of the said next day, stand vacated

(4) The power conferred on a High Court by this article shall not be in derogation of the power conferred on the Supreme Court by clause (2) of Article 32.

D. Case Studies

CASE NO. 1 Date:13/12/2020

INDIAN SEAFARERS HELP

Lessons Learned Report – 01 /2020

Grievance raised: Mr. ZuXXXXXXr Rank: TME

Subject: Fraud by unauthorised Recruitment agent at Mumbai

Incident

TME Mr. ZuXXXXXr (TME) completes GME at Chennai Based College in Aug 2019. To get a job he meets a person named Mr. XYZ (+91-83XXXXX675), a Seafarer working with a Mumbai shipping Company through his Seafarer relative NaXXXdra CXXXXa (+91-97XXXXXX01). Mr. XYZ (the agent) promises the TME to secure a job at a service charge of INR 4 lacks. Mr. XYZ works with a shipping company in Mumbai as 2nd Officer. The TME pays the advance in the anticipation of securing the job on the ship at the earliest. But the entire matter turns out to be a case of false promise and forgery. A poor Merchant Navy aspirant gets cheated and loses money (INR 1.35 lacks) to an unauthorised recruitment agent. The Trainee got a call from his college on 27 Sep 2020 for placement interview with VR Maritime (RPS MUM 199). He passed the interview and now lined up for joining ship.

Root cause and flaws in the system:

1. The TMEs are getting admission without sponsorship. They take loans to pay the fees with no surety of jobs after completion of the course.
2. Despite all the risks known to the trainees, the candidates still go to the agents because of no placement assistance given by approved 424 RPS holder companies and underperforming placement cell of MTIs.

3. Local Police do not file FIR in such cases because of which such fraudulent cases increase day by day.
4. No adequate authority with DG Shipping to take strict action against such fraudsters.

Social Impact

1. Family takes loan (upto INR 3 Lakh) to pay requisite fees at MTI. Payments to unauthorised person to get the job quickly adds up the ultimate liability of the family by another INR 4 lakh. There have been cases where family sells the property, jewellery, etc. to arrange money (INR 7 lakh) in the anticipation that one day their ward would pay all loans and help the family to lead a better life.
2. Getting into the span of such fraudulent act of unauthorised agents leads to depressive state of mind to an aspiring seafarer, who dreams for a career in Merchant Navy.

Lessons learned for others:

1. Trainee Seafarers at MTI during induction should be advised about Seafarers Rights and Grievance redressal.
2. E-gov system, RPS Rules and MLC 2006 for placement of Seafarers should be part of syllabus at MTIs.

Action taken by DG shipping: Issuance of DG

Circular: Issuance of DGS Circular 18 of 2020 dated 24/4/2020: Accordingly, Shipboard training shall be compulsory for completion of pre-sea training.

NOTE:- Victim's Name, MTI's Name, Shipping Company Names, all are replaced by fake names or different names; or hidden in order, to preserve their identity, and not to breach their Right to Privacy.

CASE NO. 2 Dated: 12/12/2020

INDIAN SEAFARERS HELP

Lessons Learned Report

Grievance raised by: Mr. Ravi (Name Changed) Rank: 4th Eng.

Incident:

4E Mr. Ravi gets an offer from non-RPS holder XXXX Group

Shipping to join an Oil Tanker MT DXXXa 98XXX24 in Iran. He pays a total INR 3.5 lacks (cash). He gets Form-I from another company named EXXXXXO TXXXXXG SXXXXXXXS PVT. LTD (RPSL CHN 53, Invalid on 03-12-2020). All documentation and cash transaction happens in CGS Shipping office. Finally, he flies to Iran from Delhi and gets in the clutch of fraudulent agents at Iran airport. The agent starts asking for money to provide the necessary clearance and final transfer to the vessel. He senses something wrong and refuses to pay money anymore. Finally, he escapes and reports to the Police. All this happens in just 7 days' time. Iran Police helps him and he is repatriated back. Presently in Kolkata. He has lodged online Grievance with DSEO Mumbai.

Root cause and flaws in the system:

1. The name of the company offering job was never an RPS holder. The candidate didn't check the DGS list of RPS agencies.
2. Payment of service-charges despite being wrong practice, was done in cash and no receipt as an acknowledgment given.
3. E-Migrate: Poor knowledge of candidate as email rec'd from sys-egovernance@dgshipping.org isn't valued.
4. RPS Module at DG Shipping data should allow PNI Cert of the ship sent to Seafarers along with E-mail.
5. No guidance to Seafarers from DG Shipping or RPS agency or Seafarers Unions / Stakeholders when Ship placement plan is changed.

Lessons learned for others:

(a) Candidates / seafarers should never get into such offers from an unauthorised agent who claims to be associated with an authorised RPS company. The candidate must check DGS portal for valid RPS agencies.

(b) Payment by cash to any agent to secure a job is illegal and against MLC rules.

(c) When RPS License is suspended, DSEO must send out alert to all Seafarers of that company by E-Gov

Action taken by DG Shipping:

RPS license of the company suspended which provided misleading information in FORM I Proposed action:

Investigation report by DESO Mumbai.

Ministry of Corporate Affairs be informed for unethical conduct of Director of the company and suspension of DIN number.

NOTE:- Victim's Name, MTI's Name, Shipping Company Names, all are replaced by fake names or different names; or hidden in order, to preserve their identity, and not to breach their Right to Privacy.

CASE NO. 3 Dated: 13/12/2020

INDIAN SEAFARERS HELP

Lessons Learned Report

Names (1) NXXXj TXXXXur (2) RXXa SXXXXXm (3) AXXXh PXXXXXl

CDC No MUM3XXXX9 MUM3XXXX4 MUM3XXXX7

Subject: Non-payment of Wages

Incident

Three seamen (as named above) get in touch with Mr. Pankaj Prabhat (Name Changed) from VRZ Maritime Pvt. Ltd. (a non RPS Holder) (Name Changed) and Mr. Rattan Pal (Name Changed) from Planet Ocean Shipping (Name Changed), RPS-MUM-3XX, for a job. They get confirmation to join a vessel named MV MXXd (IMO 7XXXXX7) in Iran. The actual vessel turns out to be a different one named as AXXXaj KXXXXn 3 (IMO-89XXXXX0). As per the contract they are to get monthly wages of USD 200 and USD 50 additional as verbal commitment by RPS. The three-seaman board the vessel and work for around a year (from July 2019 to July 2020), but gets paid only for one month.

Root cause and flaws in the system:

1. In view of no debriefing documented by DSEO during Seafarers Grievance redressal, the Human Rights abuse at Sea especially for Iran sector is running high. Hundreds are cheated this way.

2. Many Ships don't even carry PNI Cert in Iran. RPS agent can cheat any seaman and make him join him a vessel which could be unseaworthy. This may also give chance for seaman to get trapped in illegal operations of the ship and ultimately imprisonment.
3. Unawareness regarding RPS rules and Rights of Seafarers is another major cause of such increasing number of cases.
4. No legal action taken against such RPSL other than suspension of license.

Lessons learned for others:

1. Pre-Sea Training or during BST Courses, the seafarers should be given enough knowledge about their rights. When to write to DG Shipping and where to complaint if known to Seafarers, will help.
2. Despite Old DG notification on its website for being cautious in joining any vessel in Iran, candidates are still ready going and getting trapped in the unlawful activities.
3. Risks and dangers of securing job from Social websites and social media friends be made aware to Seafarers.

NOTE:- Victim's Name, MTI's Name, Shipping Company Names, all are replaced by fake names or different names; or hidden in order, to preserve their identity, and not to breach their Right to Privacy.

CASE NO. 4 Dated: 12/12/2020

INDIAN SEAFARERS HELP

Lessons Learned Report

Grievance raised by: Suresh Sharma (Name Changed)

Rank: Trainee – Diploma in Nautical Science

Incident:

Trainee Sharma completes Diploma in Nautical Science from Southern Academy of Maritime Studies in 2019. He pays INR 2,50,000 as sponsorship fees in additions to the Course fees to New Delhi based Company (RPSL MUM-4X4). Upon completion of the course the company asks to pay INR 50,000 as GST. Again, to get an early assignment, the company demands INR 42,500 as Seafarers Fund. Due to shortage of fund at home, the candidate opts not to pay the amount and waits for the assignment. But few of his colleagues pay the Seafarers fund (INR 42,500) to get an early assignment. They all happen to join a barge vessel with no proper amenities for crew. No food, no accommodation and safety gears provided to seafarers. Upon checking the details in Master Checker, nothing reflects regarding the current assignment for a month. As per his colleagues, even wages are due for payment.

Root cause and flaws in the system:

1. Part payment was done in cash with no receipt as an acknowledgement.
2. No guidance by MTIs, DG Shipping or Unions regarding the checkpoints before entering in the Employment Contract.
3. e-Migrate: Inadequate or no knowledge of e-Migrate system. In this case, the seafarers join the ship without FORM I.

Lessons learned for others:

(a) Payment by cash to any person on organisation to secure job or sponsorship is against RPS / MLC rules.

(b) The joiners must get a proper briefing and familiarisation with regard to joining vessel. Sharing the vessel details to the joiner before joining the vessel is a requirement of MS-RPS rules.

(c) Seafarers must know the process of Grievance Redressal on DG Portal.

Action Taken

No action taken against the RPS holder.

Proposed action:

Investigation report by DESO Mumbai.

Ministry of Corporate Affairs be informed for unethical conduct of Director of the company and suspension of DIN number.

NOTE:- Victim's Name, MTI's Name, Shipping Company Names, all are replaced by fake names or different names; or hidden in order, to preserve their identity, and not to breach their Right to Privacy.

CASE NO. 5

Case Study: Employer of 11 Seafarers Oman AXXXi

Shipping RPSL MUM 1X0 (Suspended on 20.06.2019), Reg No B401/MUM/PER/100+/4/8X5X4/ 2019

Mrs. Pankhuri (Name Changed) wife of Seafarer asked help from us for getting her husband and 10 other Indian Seafarers from Yemen. All Indian Seafarers are held in captivity for the last 5 months in Yemen by Armed people. Her husband calls her every once in 10 days for 2 minutes.

The Shipping company in copy has submitted attached letter to DG Shipping on 16 March 2020 stating their inability to assist the Seafarer return. Meals in captivity (Under lock): One time lunch and 2 bread pieces (Breakfast / Dinner)

Oman based Owner Ahmed Ahmed, +968 9XX3 8XX0

/ +968 9XX1 4XX6 / +967 XX4 8XX 670 / +9XX 7XX

7XX3 530.

Seafarers were sent basis Visa to Oman and not through normal RPSL clearance on Form 1. Details of one of the 11 Seafarers who are in captivity in Yemen:

Name: FXXXXz NXXXXXXn ZXXXXi Passport: K92XXXX8

FE/PE: All Legal Ports in the Sultanate

Visa No: 4XXX95/02

ARN: ER 22XXXX0

Date: 31 Jan 2020

Date of Arrest: 06 Feb 2020

Date of Contact lost as per Employer: 24 Feb 2020

Date of last contact with family: 25 July 2020

Attached Form 1 of Seaman was given to us by the

Wife of Seafarer. We doubt that it's manipulated.

Immigration clearance at Mumbai Airport: Unsure how he got. Basis Form 1 can't get.

Request for kind intervention by Indian Embassy in Oman.

NOTE:- Victim's Name, MTI's Name, Shipping Company Names, all are replaced by fake names or different names; or hidden in order, to preserve their identity, and not to breach their Right to Privacy.

CASE NO. 6

Case Study: Released from Jail on 03 May 2020 & Stranded in Iran, MV Libra, Arrested in Iran (Bandar Busher) on 02 Aug 2019, Tr Seaman Anil Kumar (Name Changed) & Bhushan (Name Chnaged), RPSL MUM 435 (OCEAN'S PRIDE MARINE) –

Incident: Both Seafarers were employed on MV Libra as per information known to family, departed India on 20.02.2019, arrested on 02 Aug 2019 and Jailed in Bandar Busher Jail. The employers Recruitment and Placement Service agency, Ocean Pride has been suspended wef 28.05.2019 and closed office and abandoned the Seafarers. Indian Agents did not pick up the phones.

Action Taken report:

Feb 2019 - Aug 22019: On Ship.

Aug 2019 - April 2019: Iranian Jail.

03 May 2020: Four Seafarers released from Jail but Master is still in Jail on the charges of Oil Smuggling.

03 May - 02 August: We were working closely with Seafarers to find a way out to get Passport which was with Iranian Navy.

Member of Parliament, Mr. Shreeniwas Patil (Sangli) about the case as he had a meeting with Father of Seafarer. Travel of Father (Farmer) from Sangli to Mumbai were arranged and met him to know all the details from DGS. Further, Seafarer was coordinated who was using Phone in Iran Jail at times. Iranian local lawyer was updating Father of the Seafarer. Since the Seafarers didn't have passport, they were staying in local flat. Moreover, a local Iranian was nominated by their friends to do all the coordination after May 2020.

Conclusion

Fresher Seafarers go through chain of agents, get into ships doing illegal activities. We propose

1. DG Shipping RPS Module for employment on IRAN/DUBAI/

MALAYSIA/TURKEY/NIGERIAN Ships should be made basis verification of data. Need to make something similar to POEA E-system for Dubai +16 other countries.

2. List of RPS agencies of Iran / UAE are known through Port and Maritime Organisation Iran and FTA Dubai respectively. IMF has been working closely with PMO on this. We suggest DG Shipping take up this issue with them. We are keen to be part of such meetings.

Scale of abuse of Human Rights at Sea:

1. Only in Iran, every year 100 Indian Seafarers get arrested / Jailed. Average age of such Seafarers is 22 Yrs old and 90% of them are freshers.
2. Unpaid wages: More than 2,000 Indian Seafarers return to India after 12 months working in Iran without wages. Wages told by Indian agents vary drastically from what Iranian Owners finally agree for Seafarers upon their arrival. Even the ships are changed, FORM 1 (DG Shipping) entries are incorrect.
3. More than 40 RPS agents and more than 150+ illegal agents are doing full time job. This includes some Iranians based in India and some Indians based in Iran.
4. Since NO INSURANCE, most of the time, Death & Disability compensation is the norm. PNI Club is fake or forged in most cases and DGS RPS Profile needs to be combed carefully.
5. In the name of Job in Iran, at least 2500 Indian Seafarers are cheated with an average of INR 3 Lakh Per Seafarer.

NOTE:- Victim's Name, MTI's Name, Shipping Company Names, all are replaced by fake names or different names; or hidden in order, to preserve their identity, and not to breach their Right to Privacy.

CASE NO. 7

Case Study: Repatriation of 4 Indian Fishermen on 11.08.2020.

Fisherman (From Tamil Nadu) were in detained by Iran Navy on 25 May 2020 & Jailed. After 68 Days court hearing they have released by court order on 02.08.2020, without fine and punishments. All arrangements done by Capt. Sanjay Prashar and team consisting of Ujjawal B. Choudhary, Mr Mehndi Navazi with the help of local

LAWYER) Financial part Airfare and consultancy charges borne by Capt. Sanjay Prashar. Fisherman Union and families borne the cost of legal fee.

Fisherman (4) names are given below.

(1) Antoni Aimai— PP No: J3475947

(2) Adlin Jeba — PP No: J6927068

(3) Adlin Gowatham— PP No: N1379536

(4) Samy Ayya — PP No: F2850716

CASE NO. 8

Case Study: Request for Repatriation of 2 Seafarers, Sharjah (Missing Passport case), stranded on-board for 19 months.

Facts of the case are:-

Captain Ashok (Name Changed) of M. X XX HXXT onboard on this vessel since May 2019. They were at Anchorage at Khwarfakkan 15 months and after that they came to know at Sharjah Anchorage that owner said the seafarers reach the port, he will arrange the signoff in short time. The ship came to Hamriyah Sharjah port on 8 October at Berth number 8. Total 8 crew was there in the ship, but 6 crew members had already been signed off on 14.12.2020.

But now the Master and AB were still onboard. Moreover, the reliever was already onboard from last 2 months. The company was telling that their passport went missing and as soon as they are found, they shall be relieved forthwith. But it's been 3 months they had not been signed off. Moreover, company stopped paying salary from October.

Action:-

The Seafarers lodged missing passport compliant on Madad.gov.in and also you may contact FTA Dubai for help. Further, they also lodged online Grievance Redressal with DG Shipping against RPSL Company.

Result:-

After lodging grievance against M.V AL HOOT in Hamariyah port inner harbour at birth no. 8 triple banks alongside with M.V SULTAN. The following were the outcomes:

1. The owner had cleared salary.
2. The new passport from embassy had been sent to the seafarers.
3. Covid-19 medical tests were also given to them and were signed off.

NOTE:- Victim's Name, MTI's Name, Shipping Company Names, all are replaced by fake names or different names; or hidden in order, to preserve their identity, and not to breach their Right to Privacy.

CASE NO. 9

Case Study: Stuck at Sharjah, Hamriya Port - C/O Harsh Vardhan DhyaniIndos: 10DLXXX4 & C/E Sanjay Singh Indos: 06YLXXX1 - RPSL Company - Vijeta Marine Services Pvt Ltd - MUM 1XX0

Brief facts of the case are:-

From past 10 months salary for the chief officer and chief engineer were kept in abeyance by the shipping company. When the seafarers informed the company, no appropriate reply was sent to them, neither any sought of communication is sent to their families by the company. Moreover, they were threatened by the agent that if they will not sail further, then they will be handed to the police. Then after the seafarers had written to the Indian Embassy Dubai and to other authorities:

DG Shipping: Grievance - GRS/SMO(M)/2020/787

MADAD - GRIEVANCE ID - UE2SFI107083320

NHRC Grievance: Diary No 11904/IN/2020

CPGRAMS Grievance - MEAPD/E/2020/03647

Scale of Abuse: The scale of abuse can be seen from the above case study, and due to lack of coordination between the authorities of India or other countries, the Human Right Abuse of Indian Seafarers are encountered numerously in different parts of the world.

NOTE:- Victim's Name, MTI's Name, Shipping Company Names, all are replaced by fake names or different names; or hidden in order, to preserve their identity, and not to breach their Right to Privacy.

CASE NO. 10

Case Study: TOTAL 58 FISHERMEN: Evacuation by Capt. Sanjay Prashar from Iran, 14/07

Here's a report

01 July 2020: Capt Sanjay Prashar rec'd call from @ L Praveen Maritime People Welfare Association Chennai Mr L Praveen, General Secretary Maritime People Welfare Association from Chennai. He got my phone number from Twitter as I have made my mobile number +91-9930467030 public.

06 July 2020: Capt Sanjay Prashar met Hon Cabinet Minister Sh. Gajendra Singh Shekhawat on the matter. I made a team of 5 and started working. Although I am working from my village in Himachal Pradesh but meeting you was very important. I returned same day to Himachal by road.

12 July 2020: Close Coordination completed with INDIAN Embassy Tehran and Fisherman. Completed list of 58 Fisherman (40 Tamil Nadu, Mainly Rameshwaram / Tuticorin and 18 Kerala).

14 July 2020 all the 58 stranded INDIAN Fisherman from Iran will be back home.

Earlier self-had brought Fisherman released from Jail in Colombo to Coimbatore by Seafarers Charter Flight.

Many Fishermen have been away from Home for more than 16 months as they had joined Iranian Fishing boats. Last 4 months due to COVID all fishing activities stopped and these Indian Fishermen were asked to go back on their own. Iranian agents refused to give them wages. No food, no wages and no International Flights, they were struggling. Every year more than 1500 Indian Fishermen from Tamil Nadu and Kerala go to Iran via Dubai to join these fishing boats. This time their agents probably had serious financial issues resulting in abuse of Human Rights at Sea. The financial cost of INR 15 Lakh to do evacuation of 58 Fisherman is borne by me. Last week also self rescued 7 INDIAN Seafarers from Iran whose passport was confiscated by Iranian agents. I had arranged financial help of INR 7 Lakh to the Stranded Seafarers as their Indian recruitment company abandoned these Seafarers. Indian Government has already brought back about 680 Fishermen by INDIAN Navy boat. We thank our government for this humane act.

These 58 Fishermen were mainly stranded at Port *assaluyah* and are being brought by Bus to Tehran, 1400 Kms Journey. It's time for Government also to think the legality of such business whereby Indians human rights are violated.

Mr Ujjwal Chaudhary from Mumbai and Mr Abu from Chennai are coordinating with Fisherman and Indian Embassy at Tehran. We are thankful to our local Iranian representative who has arranged Two Buses at his own cost just because he wants to make positive contribution for the return of Fishermen to INDIA.

CASE NO. 11

Case Study: 6 Indian Seafarers released from Jail in Iran, One Paralyzed for last 6 months, 4 more may be released today: Pathetic situation, need better response from GOI. It's for the first time that Wife of a Seaman has gone to Iran to get her husband released. Mrs. Yogini Deshpande is wife of Deck Officer Mithun and reached Tehran on 14.01.2020 to get her husband released from detention centre in Port Qeshm. She is in Port Qeshm now working to secure the release of her husband from detention centre. Ship Owner has abandoned the Seafarers. Indian Embassy response has been negative on the issue. The RPS Agency rep has also travelled with her. We hope in these final stages, atleast Indian Ambassador in Tehran will show some respect to Seafarers and assist family. Mithun and 3 others working on MT Riah were arrested on 13 July 2019 as stated in the email below. We compare this with Filipino Seafarers arrested few days from Ship and all were released after their Embassy personally took up the case with Lawyers. Philippines Govt paid fines and got their Seafarers out. Seems our Indian Embassy is so indifferent to Seafarers.

Under such extreme conditions we request a delegation including MEA officials, Shipping Industry rep and DG Shipping visit Jails and meet Seafarers to know the situation first hand. We don't know how big is the problem and what's the real cause that every month Indian Seafarers end up in Jails. Also, we suggest to investigate, why only Indian Seafarers are soft target for Iranian Authorities.

Thanks to payment of fees to Lawyer by Mrs. Yogini Deshpande and change of Lawyer that India Seafarers have been released yesterday. It seems seafarers have been left to the mercy of Families now to handle all legal help. This is unfair treatment of Seafarers as well as clear ground for Human Rights at Sea being compromised.

As reports rec'd from Iran, we hereby inform that 6 Indian Seafarers from another vessel (arrested March 2019) have been released from Jail yesterday:

(1) Navnath Salunke

(2) Sudhir Kumar

(3) Tekram Choudhari

(4) Anurag Shankar Oza

(5) Roshan Kumar Jha

(6) Pradip Vishwas

Pls note Mr Navnath got paralysis (Complete right side Body) when in Jail and last 6 months has still been languishing in Jail. He got released yesterday.

Indian Seafarers continue to be employed illegally in UAE / Iran. Every year estimated 70 Indian Seafarers get arrested in Iran on the charges of their vessels illegally plying in Iranian waters or on the charges of illegal loading / discharging of Diesel cargo.

Below 2 Iran cases of Indian Seafarers have come to our notice. We request RPS agencies be identified who had employed Indian Seafarers on OSV Venturia and MT Riah - Both arrested by Iran authorities and Indian Seafarers jailed this year. Some of the Seafarers have been released and some are still in Jail as court case proceedings are on. Most of the officers arrested have HOUNDRAS Lic and most of the ships are less than 3000 GRT.

Case 1:

Arrested on 09 May 2019 in Iran Offshore Vessel Venturia, IMO 9095814,

Ship Owner Dubai,

RPS Agency: Unknown

Self rec'd phone call from family members of two Seafarers who stated that total 8 Indian Seafarers of OSV Venturia were arrested and languishing in Iranian Jail. Last communication on WhatsApp was on 09 May 2019.

(a) Capt. Virendra INDOS No 05GL1746

(b) 2/E Rahul Kumar 09GL5455

Dubai Agent, Manoj, Ph No +971-507768583 / +971-543099777 who is in touch with family and aware of facts. The Iran Owner +964-7901348011 is not responding to the calls.

One of the family members had telephonic conversation with Indian Embassy in Tehran who confirmed that a total of 8 Seafarers were arrested and court proceedings are on.

Case 2:

Arrested on 13 July 2019 in Iran (Strait of Hormuz)

Ship Name: MT Riah

Indian Crew Manager: M/S Doris Marine Services Pvt Ltd, Mumbai, Mr Shashi Kant Ojha, Ph +91-9029169011

Ship Owner: Unknown

Technical Manager as informed by family: Black Sea General Trading LLC, Ajman,UAE,

Mr Rishi Rana, Ph No +971-508476585

Mr Jitendra Mishra, +971-501610500

Mr Amulya +971-557670351

Charges: Diesel Smuggling.

Update: Nine (9) Indian Seafarers were released on 23rd July 2019 after great effort by Indian Embassy in Tehran. Matter is undergoing judicial procedure and last hearing in the presence of 3 Seafarers as well as Lawyer in the court was on.

15.09.2019. These 9 Seafarers joined ship without e-migrate and without RPS Agency. This is a serious concern. Crew list has been submitted to your good self as separate email. Three (3) Officers are still in Jail and one of them is Mithun Deshpande. Out of three detainees, only one has joined from RPS Agency whereas other two have illegally departed India (probably on self-declaration) and ended up in Jail.

Present process followed by SEO which needs review:

Seems Indian Seafarers by-pass e-migrate system and legal recruitment or Indian Crewing agency has illegally conducted business, reference Merchant Shipping Act (Recruitment and Placement of Seafarers) Rules 2016, promulgated vide Ministry of Shipping, Govt of India Gazette Notification No GSR 169 (E) dated 15.02.2016.

There's DGS E-governance system where RPS Agency needs to upload the at least following 8 (Eight) documents and more than 32 digital entries:

1. PNI (Insurance) Certificate
2. MLC 2006 Certificate
3. DMLC Part 1
4. DMLC Part 2
5. Financial Security Document
6. CBA or SEA
7. Manning agreement between Ship Owner and Indian RPS Agency
8. Form 7 between Ship Owner and Indian RPS Agency RPS Agency then also uploads more than 32 digital entries such as, name of ship, IMO No, Official No, Flag state etc. Very much possible that e-governance system hasn't been followed by RPS agency in these cases and undue risk has been taken by RPS Agency. Any learning lessons on the case be available to Industry to avoid future such arrests of Indian Seafarers as IRAN arresting Indian Seafarers has become a norm in the name of Diesel Smuggling. No action is ever taken against PNI Clubs, SHIP Owner or Technical Manager who order such voyages and do not protect Seafarer's interests.

We are concerned at UNFAIR treatment of Seafarers as well as Criminalisation of Seafarers.

E. Conclusion and Recommendations

Human Rights on land or at sea for workers – Are they same?

Rights of Seafarer is illustrated by – "Maritime Labour Convention , 2016" (MLC) which gives:

1. Conditions of employment,
2. Facilities at workplace,
3. Social responsibility,
4. Wages,
5. Rest hours,
6. Protection and Indemnity through Insurance
7. IMO Conventions of STCW, SOLAS, MARPOL, etc. controlled technical and safety aspects.

RESPONSIBLE ENTITIES
for ensuring MLC Compliance

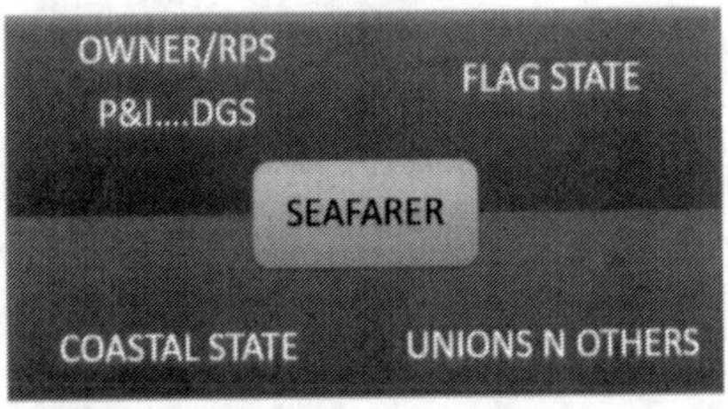

In conclusion, the following steps are suggested to address the issue of HR violations relating to the seafarers.

Curriculum for following courses should be revised by Ministry of Shipping and Indian Maritime University. It should include Seafarers rights.

(a) Personal Safety and Social Responsibility: Go beyond STCW Mandate and add Seafarers' rights issue.

(b) All 6 Pre-Sea Training Courses must have a complete chapter on E-Governance and Seafarers rights issues.

(c) Case studies should be declared to the public by DG Shipping after monthly review of ONLINE grievance redressal system.

(d) NHRC New Delhi should have quarterly meeting on Indian Seafarers rights and involve State Human Rights Commission especially Maharashtra where 90% of the fraud happens to Seafarers resulting in Human Trafficking.

(e) MEA should analyse the data on detained Indian Seafarers and involve experts in the field for their release, corrective measures and all legal interventions.

(f) Awards and rewards for those working in this field annually by NHRC can encourage more work in the field of Seafarers Rights.

(g) All Seafarers whose Human Rights have been compromised, upon return to India must be debriefed by NGO or Shipping Master. A suitable report be displayed to common man.

(h) NHRC India should take this subject with NHRC of other countries. The Seafarers Rights Bill should be introduced in every country. Unfair Treatment of Seafarers and Criminalisation of Seafarers should be deliberated at NHRC along with ILO/ IMO.

(i) More Research papers should be presented on Seafarers rights, Human Trafficking of Seafarers and cheating on a large scale ashore in India for employment of Seafarers.

E. I. Recommendations to NHRC and SHRC

I. Hold annual seminars on Seafarers rights with involvement of State Human Rights Commission.

II. Widen the grievance redressal support mechanism, that is extending it to the concerned authorities of different countries as well.

1. Ministry of Shipping: Has Online Grievance redressal system and Seafarers can report to DGCOM/ Shipping Master.
2. MEA (PGE): Reported visa MADAD.GOV.IN as well as tweet.
3. NHRC India: Recently seen some data reporting as per Industry. CPRAGMS: They direct all complaints to specific ministries.
4. NHRC of other Countries: Effective was as seen in Oman in Nov 2019.
5. NGOs, Seafarers Union: Presently highlighting the issue happens but no powers to resolve an issue.
6. **Flag state of Ship:** No Response always despite MLC 2006.

7. **Port State Control of every Country:** Not effective globally when such cases are reported. Good system in Developed countries only.
8. **ILO:** ITF reported all cases are uploaded in their website and good benchmark till Aug 2019. After DG Shipping launched online system, not required.

III. Taking the feedback of the grievance of the Indian Seafarers regularly from the authorities, and monitoring the effectiveness of the system and further, tabling the report of this effectiveness along with the improvements in the system in the Parliament / State Legislatures on quarterly basis.

IV. Publishing its monthly report of the grievance redressal mechanism on the NHRC/SHRC website regularly.

V. Moreover, by compulsorily conducting online / physicals seminars in all the Maritime Training Institutes in India, (roughly 150+ in number) on, "How to safeguard the rights of Indian Seafarers across the Globe" and educating them their rights and duties in the distress situation.

E. II. Recommendations for Ministry of Shipping, Govt. of India:

I. Conducting mandatory seminars/lectures in the field of Human Rights Education in all the maritime Training Institutes of India, educating the young minds about their Rights and How to address this evil, at the earliest.

II. Subject on "How to Address Abuse on Human Rights & Right and Duties of Indian Seafarer" should be made mandatory by Ministry of Shipping, GoI / Directorate General of Shipping, GoI; in all the Central Universities / State Universities / Private universities / Deemed Universities in India, conducting the course of Maritime Education in India.

III. Post-Sea course on the same should be made mandatory after regular interval of time, as deem fit by MoS, GoI, in order to keep the rights and duties of Indian Seafarers fresh 24×7, across the globe, wherever they work.

IV. Human Rights Course should be mandatory included in VICT course. Moreover, VICT Course, should be periodically be conducted, in order to keep the Instructors refurnished relating to the issues of Human Rights Abuse of Indian Seafarers across the Globe.

V. Submission of research work/papers/case studies on "Abuse of Human Rights of Indian Seafarers across the globe" by the head of MTI (Principles/Directors), should be made mandatory by the DGS. And benefit of the same, should be given to the MTI's during the CIP Inspection report by the DGS.

VI. In TEAP Part B, for MS(SCTW) Rules 2014: (https://www.dgshipping.gov.in/writereaddata/Shipping Notices/201911091126031424111TEA PBManual.pdf)

(a) Appendix II/4, page 175:

In Part A for the extra master's exam, EM101, Leadership, management and Human Resources should be replaced by Leadership, Management and Human Rights and Resources.

(b) Appendix – VI-2D, page 953:

Syllabus for PSSR should be revised. Chapter 6 should be revised, and Chapter 8 should be inducted on Human Rights for Indian Seafarers.

F. Case Study Relating Violation of Human Rights During Pre-Sea Training/ Post-Sea Courses

Case-1:

Case relating to a student who had been charged more by XYZ-Lines Shipping Pvt. Ltd. (RPSL MUM 000), resulting in committing fraud, harassment and loss of shipping career.

Brief facts of the case are enumerated as follows:

That a student named XYZ1(Name hidden) had completed his DNS course in July 2019 from college in Chennai. Before getting into college got sponsored by XYZ-Lines Shipping Pvt. Ltd, RPSL MUM-000, a Delhi based Shipping Company through XYZ Maritime Academy, situated in, New Delhi. He was charged about 7 Lakh Rupees (3.5 Lakh Course Fee + 3.5 Lakh Sponsorship Fees), and after completing his course, the RPSL Company neither provided job nor refunded money. That the MTI's fee was 3.5 Lakh which was clearly mentioned in the college's bona fide certificate, however, MTI was charging fee at non-uniform rate. After completing the course successfully, the student was kept in abeyance for a year and then later on, in June 2020 was sent to non-IMO approved barges by XYZ-LINES by asking more money.

Observation: From the above case, it could be seen that, the racket of RPSL fraud /crimes are gigantically increasing day-by-day, in southern part i.e., Chennai and in Northern Part i.e., Delhi as well. Moreover, strict vigil by the DGS, or MoS is required in order to explore this illegal placement services racket, which was done by some RPSL Companies and MTI's.

NOTE:- Victim's Name, MTI's Name, Shipping Company Names, all are replaced by fake names or different names; or hidden in order, to preserve their identity, and not to breach their Right to Privacy.

Case-2:

Case relating to a 3rd Engineer, of Oil Tanker treated as an un-professional/un-dignified manner at Mumbai based Academy.

Brief facts of the case are: An officer namely Ajay Kumar from engineering side, had booked his SSO course for on 05.01.2021 and was set to begin on 14.01.2021. The course was cancelled by the institute on 13.01.2021. When asked for refund, Maritime Academy at Mumbai was not willing to acknowledge it. The applicant is of the view that MTIs are Cheating and Looting officers as well. Moreover, it is alleged that the staff at these MTIs treat the officers in undignified manner, which is sheer violation of their human as well as fundamental right, i.e., Right to live with dignity.

Observation: From the above case, it is further noted that, if DGS has given a facility for booking and conducting course online, but why can't for refund online? Hence, the applicant was prejudiced by the action of Academy, thereby, violating his human right, i.e. Right to live with dignity and Right to life.

NOTE:- Victim's Name, MTI's Name, Shipping Company Names, all are replaced by fake names or different names; or hidden in order, to preserve their identity, and not to breach their Right to Privacy.

G. Case Study Relating Violation of Human Rights at Sea

Case-1:

Case relating to lack/ non-compliance of MLC 2006, due to which human rights of seafarers are curtailed.

Brief Facts of the case are: Few seafarers have been kept on board violating the MLC 2006 rules, and when the seafarers asked for sign off, they were told by the owners that, they can't relieve them as vessel cannot be left unmanned inside the port. Moreover, as per Maritime Labour Convention 2006, a seafarer can't continue more than 11 months (willingly or unwillingly). Therefore, from the above instance sheer abuse of Human Rights can be addressed.

Observation: Lack of vigil by the competent authority, due to which MLC 2006 have not been in compliance, which further lead to violation of human rights on sea.

NOTE:- Victim's Name, MTI's Name, Shipping Company Names, all are replaced by fake names or different names; or hidden in order, to preserve their identity, and not to breach their Right to Privacy.

Case-2:

Case of Indian Sailors Detained in Iran - 11 Crew Members

Brief facts of the case are: On the 15th of May, 2020, MSV Qr-alfaz (registration M.N.V. 1XX1) set off from Dubai UAE, toward Karachi, in Pakistan with a cargo of electronic goods. While in international waters, they were arrested by the Iranian coast guard and taken to Qeshm jail. The authorities in Iran have charged them for smuggling (under Articles 28 and 29 of the Anti-Smuggling Act of Iran) and have seized the vessel, goods, and all 11 seafarers. The fine set by the court for freeing the seafarers is over 3,00,000 AED, which is way beyond any sum they can afford. At this point, the crew has been in jail since May, first on Qeshm Island, from where they have been transferred to Sarad Jail in Bander Abbas as of November 22, 2020. The families of these seafarers are as one can imagine, completely distraught. They are not educated and have had difficulties communicating in both Farsi, and English.

The seafarers on board this vessel for over 10 years, and desperate to find assistance for them and their families. The families have also written to authorities in India, but have not received any response despite repeated efforts.

They were sailing to Karachi from Dubai with Cargo loads with Electrical items before they reach Karachi they were attacked by Iranian Pirates. On the same time Iran Navy reported and arrested all of them including Iranian Pirates. They all were taken to Qesham Island and kept them including pirates for 5 months. Later on Pirates were released and rest crew total in 11 were put on jail in Bhandar Abbas (Iran) 5 days before. Mr. Imran they have requested a lot to Indian Embassy but no help was been done.

As per Mr. Imran stated Iran Govt asked to release all 11 crew family members by paying fine is AED 25000 per person, or roughly INR 5,04,000. They have no information about their boat location and the condition of the boat. Above incident happened in the month of May 2020.

Observation: Lack of Co-ordination among dept/s, ministries of India and other Countries.

NOTE:- Victim's Name, MTI's Name, Shipping Company Names, all are replaced by fake names or different names; or hidden in order, to preserve their identity, and not to breach their Right to Privacy.

Case-3:

Case of 5 Indian Seafarers sent to Prison in Nigeria, MV Bounty, Flag Vanuatu, IMO 71XXX47, on ground that they were involved in illegal trading.

Brief facts of the case are: Chief Engineer was stranded on MV Bounty in Nigeria from 31 Jan 2020. Their ship came for repairs and AIS was switched off. Nigerian Navy boarded the ship and took away

3 Indian Seafarers and lodged them in Jail. There's no cargo on-board. Furthermore, all these 5 Seafarers went by self-declaration in e-migrate system and thus no RPSL involved in their placement. They flew from Chandigarh Airport and joined in Morocco. Total crew is 5 only. Chief Engineer and Cook were on Ship whereas; Capt., Chief Officer and 2/E are in Jail from 31 Jan 2020.

Crew in Lagos Ikoyi Prison. Four weeks ago, Nigerian Navy took the crew from ship and send them to Efcc cell. After court hearing they were granted bail on stipulation that we should arrange 5 Nigerian and 5 Indian Citizen, for witness. Further, our company requested to Indian Embassy to arrange 5 Indian Citizen. Till today's date, no person has been arranged by Competent Authority, failure of which those 5 Indian Seafarers shall be sent to jail Lagos Ikoyi. Moreover, no ground was put on record, for their detention; hence their detention was illegal under eyes of law.

Observation: Due to lack of co-ordination among competent authorities, rights of Seafarers are languished.

NOTE:- Victim's Name, MTI's Name, Shipping Company Names, all are replaced by fake names or different names; or hidden in order, to preserve their identity, and not to breach their Right to Privacy.

Case-4:

Case of Indian Seafarer stranded in Nigeria (Jailed earlier) from 19 April 2019 (Mr. SaXXXr RXX JarXXXXX, INDOS 1XHLXXX1), returns after 2 years.

HYDERABAD: A 26-year-old seafarer from Andhra Pradesh, who has been detained for 17 months in Nigeria after his ship's unauthorised entry to the country's waters, has reached the Indian high commission in Abuja. The seafarer was brought to Abuja by an official of the commission from Port Hart Court.

He was on Bonny Island after their vessel MT ApXXXs was seized by the authorities in April 2019. He escaped from being captured by Somalian pirates. Social worker from Chennai and community development manager of 'Sailors Society' Captain MXXXX, who was following up on the seafarer's detention, told TOI that the seafarer was finally brought out of the ship and given a temporary passport by the high commission.

Mumbai-based social worker SXXXX MXXXX, got a reply from the ship captain that they were prepared to hand over the seafarer to the Indian authorities since he was out on bail. SXXXXX followed up the matter with the Indian high commission and also arranged for food supplies to seafarer, who was stranded on the ship.

In the meantime, Captain SaXXXy PrXXXXr of International Maritime Federation gave a detailed account of the incidents leading up to the ship's seizure to the director general of shipping and ministry of external affairs with a plea that the seafarer must be helped to return to AP. He termed Rao's arrest as "criminalisation" of seafarers.

Release of Indian Seafarer, from Ship MT ApXXXXs (Nigerian Waters) and return to India.

It will be a great help if Indian DG Shipping talks to Nigerian NIMSA (Nigerian Maritime Administration and Safety) on the subject matter. We understand that this is a clear case of "Unfair Treatment of Seafarers and Criminalisation of Seafarers". A Seafarer who makes a brave attempt to save himself from Pirates is jailed and it's been 15.5 months now. He is stranded onboard Ship from Dec 2019 onwards and needs to be given all the help from Seafarers Welfare Fund Society (SWFS).

Observation: From the above case it can be observed the high handedness of authorities in protecting the rights of Indian Seafarers.

NOTE:- Victim's Name, MTI's Name, Shipping Company Names, all are replaced by fake names or different names; or hidden in order, to preserve their identity, and not to breach their Right to Privacy.

Case-5:

Case of Late Saurabh Kumar INDOS 18GL6368 (Malaysia Sibu), RPSL Vijeta MUM 1020. 106

Rev 06, Date 24 Jan 2021

Brief Facts of the case are: (Saurabh Kumar), CDC No MUM365544, was working on vessel (TB Global 1) as per Indian DG Shipping record, IMO number (9742182), INDOS NO 18GL6368 currently operating in Malaysia. On 24th July 2020 at around afternoon 12:30 pm, Malaysian time while doing chipping work on the forward hull of ship, he slipped and fell in the river. As the reports came to me (Capt. Sanjay Prashar), his co-worker Vinay Whatsaap Contact (+91-6239034153) immediately went for help, but due to current, he had already flown away to the aft of the vessel. Search craft went but couldn't find him. Neither the Indian agency (Vijeta Marine Services) who sent him, nor the Malaysian agency Makira Marine were updating me about the current status. After this I started tweeting to embassy shipping minister in twitter, after my several tweet Shipping Minister Shri. Mansukh Mandviya sir, replied "As soon as we got a note about the incident DG Shipping got in touch with MEA India and Indian Embassy @hcikl to get the matter investigated, already in touch with authorities and keep you updated." This he replied to our tweet. During the period of 24th July 2020 till 26th July 2020, I was in touch with the DG shipping, but they were unable to trace the ship's location, so they asked me if I can ask his friend Vinay who was working with my brother in the same ship to share the location. I did and things worked successfully, meanwhile, doing all these I got to know that according to the record of DG shipping he was working on TB Global 1 ship, but he was not working on that ship, he has been transferred to some other ship MV TUNG WANG BARU, when my brother reached to Malaysia, the Malaysian agent Nicolas told him that there is no vacancy in TB Global 1 so he asked him to join a costal ship MV TUNG WANG BARU which doesn't even have IMO registration, Malaysian agent told my brother that, after completion of his job, the agent will give him stamp of an IMO ship, I want to mention my brother Late Saurabh Kumar was sailing for the first time, he has no idea regarding the terms, and also from Vijeta Marine RPSL company from which he has been send to Malaysia on 26th Sep 2019, Licence of Vijeta Marine was suspended after 5 days the day he left for Malaysia. And owner of Vijeta Marine is missing since then. The day when my brother left India on 26th Sep 2019 a day before a Declaration was signed by him and by my parents which I had shared in the document, where it was clearly mentioned that in case of any death and accidental Makira marine is not responsible. This was done at the last moment.

Observation: It is observed from the above case that, human trafficking and cheating were done to youngsters, as freshers gets into their trap. After investigating, I got to know that Makira marine has their branch in Pakkar Kerala, and they have their own shipping in Sarawak Malaysia. Two Agents were involved in this. Indian Agent

AkhilKrishnan 9656814294, Malaysian Agent Nicholas +6016-8568877.

On 26th of July 2020 I (Capt. Sanjay Prashar) got confirmation from the DG shipping about the death of the young seafarer. After several efforts from the family side, we received his mortal remains in India on 13th Aug 2020 11:30pm to New Delhi and then it was further transported to Patna Airport on 14th August 2020 5:30am.

"According to the record of DG shipping, Late Saurabh Kumar was working on Ship TB Global. Actually, he was not working on that ship as he was transferred to another ship MV TUNG WANG BARU. When Late Saurabh Kumar reached Malaysia on 20 Sept 2019, the Malaysian Agent Nicolas Ph no +60-168568877 told him that there is no vacancy in TB Global 1, so he asked him to join a coastal ship MV TUNG WANG BARU. The coastal ships didn't have IMO registration. Malaysian agent told my late Saurabh Kumar that, after completion of his job, the agent will give him a stamp of an IMO ship.

H. Case Study Relating Violation of Human Rights at Shore

Case-1:

Case relating to lack of co-ordination between the departments / ministries / and foreign embassies, due to which rights of a seafarer.

Brief Facts of the case are:

That I (Wife) received a call from my husband Mr. Ajay Pardeshi on 09/11/2019. After 10 days on 18/11/2019 evening one of Ajay's friend called over phone and informed that Ajay has been arrested by Sydney police (Australia). No one from the company informed the family about the situation. That on 18th November, I (Wife) received a call from fellow seafarer informing that Mr. Ajay Pardeshi was arrested and signed off from the ship. He also asked if the family was informed about any incident by the Royal Caribbean (RPS agent). We were surprised to know that that despite asking multiple times we were not informed about any information or the incident occurred onboard.

We contacted Hiren International RPSLMUM- 2019 on 19th Nov 2019, and we were advised by Mr. Hiren to send an email to Royal Caribbean Manning India Pvt. Ltd. (RCM) crewassist@rccl.com. Upon sending email to crewassist@rccl.com, we were informed that Mr. Ajay Pardeshi had already signed-off from the vessel on 12th November and it was also mentioned that the RPS company would come back to us if Mr. Ajay Pardeshi arranged his own travel arrangement back to India or not.

We contacted many authorities like, MEA, POEA, ACP and PIC of RCM to know the whereabouts of my husband Mr. Ajay Pardeshi but no firm information provided by any source. We also contacted Bureau of Immigration to check when Mr. Ajay Pardeshi took flight to India, but again no firm information received. With our resources on

20th November, we got to know that Mr. Ajay Pardeshi has been arrested and kept at Parklea Correctional Centre, Sydney. On 22nd November, we officially raised a complaint to POEA(MEA), Mumbai. On 26th November. I received a phone call from Community, Sydney (MEA) informing us that some official was going to meet Mr. Ajay Pardeshi in the Correctional Centre and I was asked for any message to be given to him. On 28th November, we were officially informed by Community, Sydney (MEA) about the charges against my husband Mr. Ajay Pardeshi vide email. As per the email, we as family members were advised to appoint a lawyer who can represent the case. It was also mentioned that plea of bail was also rejected due to non-availability of Australian address. The date of hearing mentioned in the email is 08/01/2020. We were also given details of 3 nos. Lawyer and advised to select one of them. We contacted Mr. Mohan Sundar (+61 2 96797000) and he advised us to reach out to another lawyer who was never contactable. Then we contacted Ms. Nyman Gibson Miralis (+61 – 2 9264 8884) but again due to language barrier we could not make her understand about our queries. Neither, we were able to understand her clearly. She noted our contact details and advised us that she was going to call us back. Till date no information received from her end. Another lawyer Mr. Mittu Gopalan (+61-2 8917 8700) was not reachable on the given number.

Now we are in touch and with POEA (MEA) and seeking guidance to proceed in this case. On their advice and intervention of IMF representative, today (02/12/2019) we have requested RCM to furnish some basic information pertaining to employment of Mr. Ajay Pardeshi, which would help us in dealing the case legally. Now we are waiting for the information from Mr. John D’souza (General Manager) (+91-8291920242) RCM (RPS agent). I shall keep you posted with outcome on regular basis.

Observation: From the above case, it could be noted that if there is firm co-ordination between the departments / ministries / and foreign embassy’s then, human rights of a seafarer could not be violated.

I. Methods to Report Human Rights Abuses

RIGHTS ABUSES:

1. Grievance Redressal Mechanism (Online).
2. Filing a complaint to NHRC / SHRC.
3. Writing to Dept of Personnel and Training.
4. Seeking support of Seafarers' National/International Union.
5. Last but not the least, knocking the door of judiciary, District Court(s) of respective states, Hon'ble High Court(s) of respective states, and Hon'ble Supreme Court of India.

Index

V

W

Y